Authors:
Patricia Carratello, M.A.
Mentor Teacher

John Carratello, M.A.
Mentor Teacher

Illustrator:
Keith Vasconcelles

Contributing Editor:
Evan D. Forbes, M.S. Ed.

Editor:
Walter Kelly, M.A.

Senior Editor:
Sharon Coan, M.S. Ed.

Art Director:
Darlene Spivak

Product Manager:
Phil Garcia

Imaging:
Rick Chacón

Publishers:
Rachelle Cracchiolo, M.S. Ed.
Mary Dupuy Smith, M.S. Ed.

Hands-On Minds-On Science

Animals

Teacher Created Materials

Teacher Created Materials, Inc.
P.O. Box 1040
Huntington Beach, CA 92647
©1994 Teacher Created Materials, Inc.
Made in U.S.A.

ISBN-1-55734-626-7

Table of Contents

Table of Contents *(cont.)*

Introduction

What Is Science?

What is science to young children? Is it something that they know is a part of their world? Is it a textbook in the classroom? Is it a tadpole changing into a frog? Is it a sprouting seed, a rainy day, a boiling pot, a turning wheel, a pretty rock, or a moonlit sky? Is science fun and filled with wonder and meaning? What does science mean to children?

Science offers you and your eager children opportunities to explore the world around you and to make connections between the things you experience. The world becomes your classroom, and you, the teacher, a guide.

Science can, and should, fill children with wonder. It should cause them to be filled with questions and the desire to discover the answers to their questions. And, once they have discovered the answers, they should be actively seeking new questions to answer!

The books in this series give you and your children the opportunity to learn from the whole of your experience—the sights, sounds, smells, tastes, and touches, as well as what you read, write about, and do. This whole science approach allows you to experience and understand your world as you explore science concepts and skills together.

What Are Animals?

When you think of animals, what comes to mind–dogs, cats, maybe a cute little bunny? When asked about animals, the majority of people think of the ones that have been domesticated throughout the world. In actuality, domesticated animals make up only a small percentage of animals worldwide. In society's not-so-distant past, wild animals, which have always been more abundant than domesticated animals, were often regarded as pests and killers of livestock. Examples are locusts, wolves, and grizzly bears. It is only in the last ten years or so that the plight of animals, domestic and wild alike, is being realized by people worldwide. Research is beginning to show just how important animals are to the well-being of our own lives. And, since certain species of animals are indicators of the environment around us, it is becoming increasingly important that we learn about what animals have to offer.

Scientists have categorized every animal that has been identified to date into one of seven classes (amphibians, arthropods, birds, fish, mammals, mollusks, and reptiles). A class is defined as a group of animals that have similar characteristics. For example, warm-blooded animals are in the class of mammals. Throughout this book you will have the opportunity to study and learn about animals, both domestic and wild, that are in these seven classes.

The Scientific Method

The scientific method is a creative and systematic process for proving or disproving a given question, following an observation. When scientists use the scientific method, a basic set of guiding principles and procedures is followed in order to obtain new knowledge about our universe. This method will be described in the paragraphs that follow.

It is easy to teach the scientific method! Just follow these simple steps:

 Make an **OBSERVATION**.

The teacher presents a situation, gives a demonstration, or reads background material that interests students and prompts them to ask questions. Or students can make observations and generate questions on their own as they study a topic.

Example: An owl pellet sitting on a table.

 Select a **QUESTION** to investigate.

In order for students to select a question for a scientific investigation, they will have to consider the materials they have or can get, as well as the resources (books, magazines, people, etc.) actually available to them. You can help them make an inventory of their materials and resources, either individually or as a group.

Tell students that in order to successfully investigate the questions they have selected, they must be very clear about what they are asking. Discuss effective questions with your students. Depending upon their level, simplify the question or make it more specific.

Example: How do birds of prey (eagles, hawks, owls, etc.) digest their food?

 Make a **PREDICTION** *(Hypothesis)*.

Explain to students that a hypothesis is a good guess about what the answer to a question will probably be. But they do not want to make just any old guess. Encourage students to predict what they think will happen and why.

In order to formulate a hypothesis, students may have to gather more information through research.

Have students practice making hypotheses with questions you give them. Tell them to pretend they have already done their research. What you want to have them do is write each hypothesis so it follows these rules:

    1. It is to the point.
    2. It tells what will happen, based on what the question asks.
    3. It follows the subject/verb relationship of the question.

Example: I think birds of prey eat their food whole and digest what they can.

The Scientific Method *(cont.)*

 Develop a **PROCEDURE** to test the hypothesis.

The first thing students must do in developing a procedure (the test plan) is to determine the materials they will need.

They must state exactly what needs to be done in step-by-step order. If they do not place their directions in the right order, or if they leave out a step, it becomes difficult for someone else to follow their directions. A scientist never knows when other scientists will want to try the same experiment to see if they end up with the same results!

Example: Using an owl pellet, you will examine it to determine what happened to the animal eaten.

 Record the **RESULTS** of the investigation in written and picture form.

The results (data collected) of a scientific investigation are usually expressed two ways—in written form and in picture form. Both are summary statements. The written form reports the results with words. The picture form (often a chart or graph) reports the results so the information can be understood at a glance.

Example: The results of the investigation can be recorded on a data-capture sheet provided (page 17).

 State a **CONCLUSION** that tells what the results of the investigation mean.

The conclusion is a statement which tells the outcome of the investigation. It is drawn after the student has studied the results of the experiment, and it interprets the results in relation to the stated hypothesis. A conclusion statement may read something like either of the following: "The results show that the hypothesis is supported," or "The results show that the hypothesis is *not* supported." Then restate the hypothesis if it was supported or revise it if it was not supported.

Example: The hypothesis that stated "birds of prey eat their food whole and digest what they can" is supported (or not supported).

 Record **QUESTIONS, OBSERVATIONS,** and **SUGGESTIONS** for future investigations.

Students should be encouraged to reflect on the investigations that they complete. These reflections, like those of professional scientists, may produce questions that will lead to further investigations.

Example: What other animals eat their food whole?

Science-Process Skills

Even the youngest students blossom in their ability to make sense out of their world and succeed in scientific investigations when they learn and use the science-process skills. These are the tools that help children think and act like professional scientists.

The first five process skills on the list below are the ones that should be emphasized with young children, but all of the skills will be utilized by anyone who is involved in scientific study.

Observing

It is through the process of observation that all information is acquired. That makes this skill the most fundamental of all the process skills. Children have been making observations all their lives, but they need to be made aware of how they can use their senses and prior knowledge to gain as much information as possible from each experience. Teachers can develop this skill in children by asking questions and making statements that encourage precise observations.

Communicating

Humans have developed the ability to use language and symbols which allow them to communicate, not only in the "here and now," but over time and space as well. The accumulation of knowledge in science, as in other fields, is due to this process skill. Even young children should be able to understand the importance of researching others' communications about science and the importance of communicating their own findings in ways that are understandable and useful to others. The animal journal and the data-capture sheets used in this book are two ways to develop this skill.

Comparing

Once observation skills are heightened, students should begin to notice the relationships between things that they are observing. Comparing means to notice the similarities and differences. By asking how things are alike and different, or which is smaller or larger, for example, teachers will encourage children to develop their comparison skills.

Ordering

Other relationships that students should be encouraged to observe are the linear patterns of seriation (order along a continuum: e.g., rough to smooth, large to small, bright to dim, few to many) and sequence (order along a time line or cycle). By making graphs, time lines, cyclical and sequence drawings, and by putting many objects in order by a variety of properties, students will grow in their abilities to make precise observations about the order of nature.

Categorizing

When students group or classify objects or events according to logical rationale, they are using the process skill of categorizing. Students begin to use this skill when they group by one property such as color. As they develop this skill, they will be attending to multiple properties in order to make categorizations. The animal classification system, for example, is one system students can categorize.

Science-Process Skills *(cont.)*

Relating

Relating, which is one of the higher level process skills, requires student scientists to notice how objects and phenomena interact with one another and the changes caused by these interactions. An obvious example of this is the study of chemical reactions.

Inferring

Not all phenomena are directly observable, because they are out of humankind's reach in terms of time, scale, and space. Some scientific knowledge must be logically inferred based on the data that is available. Much of the work of paleontologists, astronomers, and those studying the structure of matter is done by inference.

Applying

Even very young, budding scientists should begin to understand that people have used scientific knowledge in practical ways to change and improve the way we live. It is at this application level that science becomes meaningful for many students.

Organizing Your Unit

Designing a Science Lesson

In addition to the lessons presented in this unit, you will want to add lessons of your own, lessons that reflect the unique environment in which you live, as well as the interests of your students. When designing new lessons or revising old ones, try to include the following elements in your planning:

Question

Pose a question to your students that will guide them in the direction of the experience you wish to perform. Encourage all answers, but you want to lead the students toward the experience you are going to be doing. Remember, there must be an observation before there can be a question. (Refer to The Scientific Method, pages 5-6.)

Setting the Stage

Prepare your students for the lesson. Brainstorm to find out what students already know. Have children review books to discover what is already known about the subject. Invite them to share what they have learned.

Materials Needed for Each Group or Individual

List the materials each group or individual will need for the investigation. Include a data-capture sheet when appropriate.

Procedure

Make sure students know the steps to take to complete the activity. Whenever possible, ask them to determine the procedure. Make use of assigned roles in group work. Create (or have your students create) a data-capture sheet. Ask yourself, "How will my students record and report what they have discovered? Will they tally, measure, draw, or make a checklist? Will they make a graph? Will they need to preserve specimens?" Let students record results orally, using a video or audio tape recorder. For a written recording, encourage students to use a variety of paper supplies such as poster board or index cards. It is also important for students to keep a journal of their investigation activities. Journals can be made of lined and unlined paper. Students can design their own covers. The pages can be stapled or put together with brads or spiral binding.

Extensions

Continue the success of the lesson. Consider which related skills or information you can tie into the lesson, like math, language arts skills, or something being learned in social studies. Make curriculum connections frequently and involve the students in making these connections. Extend the activity, whenever possible, to home investigations.

Closure

Encourage students to think about what they have learned and how the information connects to their own lives. Prepare animal journals using "Animal Journal" directions on page 80. Provide an ample supply of blank and lined pages for students to use as they complete the "Closure" activities. Allow time for students to record their thoughts and pictures in their journals.

Organizing Your Unit *(cont.)*

Structuring Student Groups for Scientific Investigations

Using Cooperative Learning strategies in conjunction with hands-on and discovery learning methods will benefit all of the students taking part in the investigation.

Cooperative Learning Strategies

1. In cooperative learning all group members need to work together to accomplish the task.

2. Cooperative learning groups should be heterogeneous.

3. Cooperative learning activities need to be designed so that each student contributes to the group and individual group members can be assessed on their performance.

4. Cooperative learning teams need to know the social as well as the academic objectives of a lesson.

Cooperative Learning Groups

Groups can be determined many ways for the scientific investigations in your class. Here is one way of forming groups that has proven to be successful in primary classrooms.

- **The Expedition Leader**—scientist in charge of reading directions and setting up equipment.
- **The Zoologist**—scientist in charge of carrying out directions (can be more than one student).
- **The Stenographer**—scientist in charge of recording all of the information.
- **The Transcriber**—scientist who translates notes and communicates findings.

If the groups remain the same for more than one investigation, require each group to vary the people chosen for each job. All group members should get a chance to try each job at least once.

Using Centers for Scientific Investigations

Set up stations for each investigation. To accommodate several groups at a time, stations may be duplicated for the same investigation. Each station should contain directions for the activity, all necessary materials (or a list of materials for investigators to gather), a list of words (a word bank) which students may need for writing and speaking about the experience, and any data-capture sheets or materials needed for recording and reporting data and findings.

Station-to-Station Activities are on pages 69-78. Model and demonstrate each of the activities for the whole group. Have directions at each station. During the modeling session, have a student read the directions aloud while the teacher carries out the activity. When all students understand what they must do, let small groups conduct the investigations at the centers. You may wish to have a few groups working at the centers, while others are occupied with other activities. In this case, you will want to set up a rotation schedule so all groups have a chance to work at the centers.

Assign each team to a station, and after they complete the task described, help them rotate in a clockwise order to the other stations. If some groups finish earlier than others, be prepared with another unit-related activity to keep students focused on main concepts.

After all rotations have been made by all groups, come together as a class to discuss what was learned.

Just the Facts

You have lived all your life surrounded by animals. But, do you know what an animal is?

An animal is a living thing. It starts small and if it gets the things it needs to grow, it grows larger. But, unlike a plant, an animal must eat other things to live since it cannot produce its own food inside its body.

Most animals have six systems--RESPIRATORY, DIGESTIVE, CIRCULATORY, LOCOMOTIVE, REPRODUCTIVE, and PERCEPTIVE. Each system has a job to do in helping an animal live and grow.

- RESPIRATORY SYSTEM—All animals breathe oxygen. They must breathe to stay alive. Some animals have lungs, while others have gills, and some absorb oxygen through the skin.
- DIGESTIVE SYSTEM—All animals eat something. Some eat plants, some eat other animals, and some eat both plants and animals. Once animals eat food, they need to digest it and get rid of the parts their bodies do not use.
- CIRCULATORY SYSTEM—The food the animal eats and the oxygen it breathes need to be carried to all parts of the animal's body. Most animals have hearts that pump the blood that carries the food and oxygen to all the cells in the body so the cells can live and grow.
- LOCOMOTIVE SYSTEM—Animals need to be able to move around to find food, escape from their predators, and find a good place to live. Some animals have legs and feet, such as humans and cats. Others also have wings, such as birds and insects. Some just use muscles and wriggle their bodies, such as fish, worms, and snails.
- REPRODUCTIVE SYSTEM—All animals have offspring. Some lay eggs, while others give birth to live young. If animals did not have babies, very soon that species of animal would disappear.
- PERCEPTIVE SYSTEM—Animals need some way to be aware of their environment. Most animals have sensory perception (the use of their eyes, ears, nose, and senses of touch and taste). These senses allow them to find food, safety, and shelter.

There are two major divisions in the animal kingdom: animals with backbones and animals without. Animals with backbones or vertebrae are called vertebrates. They include amphibians, birds, fish, mammals, and reptiles. All have skeletons that support their bodies and help them move around. Animals without backbones or vertebrae are called invertebrates. They include arthropods (such as insects, lobsters, and spiders), corals, jellyfish, mollusks (such as clams and snails), sea urchins, starfish, sponges, and worms. Of all the millions of animals that exist in the world today, the majority are invertebrates.

Find It

Questions

Define the word *diversity*. How much animal diversity is present in everyday life?

Setting the Stage

- Have students compare their ideas of what an animal is with the ideas of others in the class.
- Discuss with students various kinds of animals such as amphibians, arthropods, birds, corals, fish, jellyfish, mammals, mollusks, reptiles, sea urchins, starfish, sponges, and worms.
- Have students create a list of all the animals they saw on the way to school today.
- Discuss with students ways to observe animals without harming them.

Materials Needed for Each Individual

- pencil and paper
- data-capture sheet (page 13)

Procedure *(Student Instructions)*

1. Walk around the school yard looking for different kinds of animals.

2. On your data-capture sheet, write down the name or draw a picture of each animal that you find, including the type of animal it is. For example, a cat is a mammal and a lizard is a reptile.

3. Write two descriptive words for each animal. Each descriptive word may be used only once during the investigation.

4. Consolidate all student lists into one list on the board.

5. List animals by their types.

6. Determine which type of animal was seen most.

7. Work together as a class to come up with a list of traits all animals have in common.

Extensions

- Have students use a camera to take pictures of the animals to compare and classify in class.

Closure

In their animal journals, have students write their ideas of what an animal is. Have each student draw a picture of their favorite animal seen.

12

Find It *(cont.)*

Complete the chart below.

Name of Animal	Type of Animal	Picture of Animal	2 Descriptive Words

Take a Breath

Questions

How do animals breathe? What is lung capacity? How can it be measured?

Setting the Stage

- Discuss with students the process of the lungs.
- Ask students if all animals breathe the same way.
- Ask students if the size of an animal relates to its lung capacity.

Materials Needed for Each Group

- one gallon (4000 mL) plastic bottle
- large bowl
- plastic tubing
- two screw-on bottle tops
- masking tape
- marking pen
- data-capture sheet (page 15)

Procedure *(Student Instructions)*

1. Using masking tape and marking pen, divide bottle into quarters.

2. Fill large bowl and one gallon (4000 mL) plastic bottle with water.

3. Place bowl of water on the table. Then turn plastic bottle upside down with your hand covering the top and place it inside the bowl, top side down, making sure to remove your hand.

4. Place two bottle tops underneath the mouth of the bottle, supporting it in the water and making enough room to insert the plastic tubing into the bottle.

5. Insert one end of the plastic tubing into the bottle, leaving enough tubing for it to rest on the outside of the bowl.

6. Take a deep breath and **exhale** into the plastic tube. Make sure you do not inhale through the tube.

7. Measure the remaining amount of water in the bottle and record on a data-capture sheet. Repeat this process until you get two equal measurements.

Extensions

- Have students draw a diagram of the human respiratory system and explain to them how breathing takes place.
- Have students, at home, compare the breathing between a cat and a dog. Then, have them compare the breathing between the cat, the dog, and themselves. When comparing breathing, things to look for are rapidity of breath, chest expansion, and nose-mouth use.

Closure

In their animal journals, have students draw the respiratory system of an amphibian, fish, and a mammal.

Take a Breath *(cont.)*

Record the remaining water amounts.

Student Name	Water Measurement

In your group, who had the least water left in the bottle? _____

Who had the most? _____

Why? _____

_____

In your entire class, who had the least water left in the bottle? _____

Who had the most? _____

Why? _____

_____

What's Left?

Question

How do birds of prey (eagles, hawks, and owls) digest their food?

Setting the Stage

- Prior to this activity, ask students to think about how they would eat if they did not have teeth. How big a piece of food could you swallow whole, without any chewing? What foodstuffs could you not eat?

- Point out to students that birds do not have any teeth. Ask them what kinds of things birds eat. How do they eat these things?

- Explain to students that birds of prey swallow things whole and then cough up the parts of animals they cannot digest.

Materials Needed for Each Group

- plastic gloves
- tray or waxed paper sheet
- tweezers
- magnifying glass and/or other instruments for exploration
- owl pellets (fumigated), commercially available
- data-capture sheet (page 17)

Procedure *(Student Instructions)*

1. Put on plastic gloves.
2. Place owl pellet on tray.
3. Using tweezers, carefully pull apart the pellet.
4. Separate the various parts of the pellet and place in the appropriate place on the data-capture sheet.

Extensions

- Have students discuss what was found in the various pellets. Why could the owl not digest these parts? What do we do with the parts of plants and animals that we cannot digest?

Closure

In their animal journals, have students describe what it was like to pull apart the owl pellet. What did they think while they did it? Now, have them describe what their life would be like if they had to cough up all the things they could not digest—especially in front of other people!

16

What's Left? *(cont.)*

Glue the bones you find in the appropriate places.

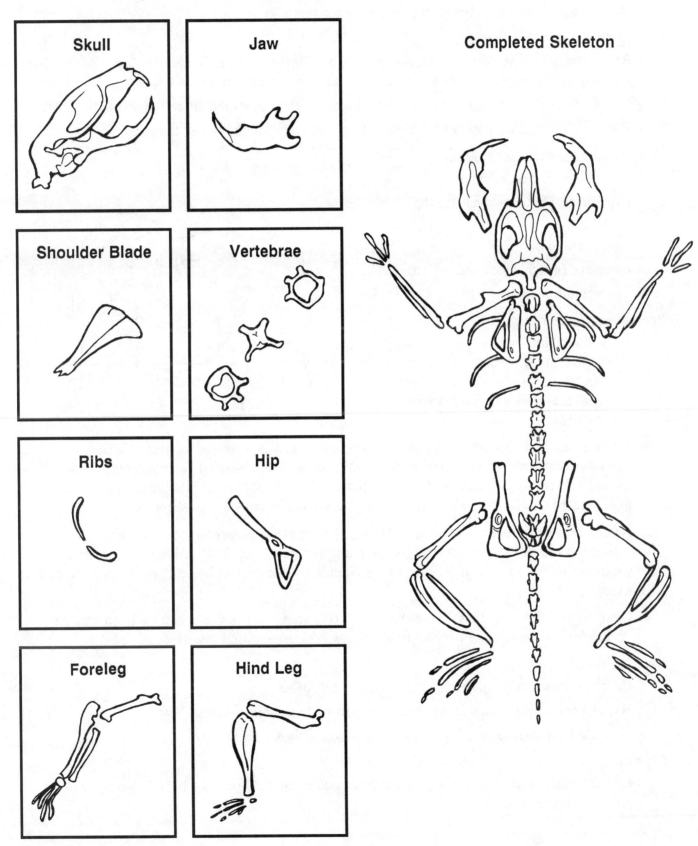

| Skull | Jaw | Completed Skeleton |

Shoulder Blade   Vertebrae

Ribs   Hip

Foreleg   Hind Leg

Listen to your Heart

Question

> What vital function does the heart perform for all animals?

Setting the Stage

- Review with your students the circulatory system of several classes of animals (amphibians, fish, reptiles, and mammals). Have them look for similarities and differences in each animal's system.
- Using a large diagram of the human heart, discuss with students the different parts of the heart.
- Discuss with students how the heart pumps food and oxygen throughout the body.

Materials Needed for Each Group

- 3 feet (1 m) of rubber tuning
- two funnels (You could use the tops of plastic bottles.)
- masking tape
- timepiece (watch, clock, stopwatch, etc.)
- data-capture sheet (page 19), one per student

Procedure *(Student Instructions)*

1. Insert funnel into one end of the plastic tubing. Secure it with masking tape. Attach the second funnel to the other end of the tubing in the same way. This is your stethoscope.

2. While at rest, put one end of stethoscope to your ear and the other end against your heart. Listen. After you have listened to your heart for a while, count the number of beats you feel in 15 seconds. Multiply the number of beats by four, and that is your heart rate (beats per minute) at rest. Record the number in the appropriate column on the data-capture sheet.

3. Next, run in place for about a minute. Using the stethoscope, listen to your heart beat for 15 seconds, counting the number of beats and multiplying by four. That number is your heart rate (beats per minute) after activity. Record the number in the appropriate column on the data-capture sheet.

4. Compare the numbers at rest to the numbers during activity. See if you can come up with any conclusions about how the circulatory system works during different periods of activity.

Extensions

- Have students pick partners and listen to their heart beats.
- Have students bring in a real stethoscope and listen to an animal's heart beat.
- Have students compare the heart beats of a person to those of an animal.

Closure

> In their animal journals, have students draw an outline of the human body and identify the pulse points with dots or stars.

Listen to Your Heart *(cont.)*

Record the information from the experience below.

Name	🧎 Resting 🧎	🏃 Running 🏃

Conclusions about experience: _____

_____

_____

Do the Locomotion

Question

How do fish and other finned aquatic animals move in the water?

Setting the Stage

- Ask students to list all the possible ways animals can move around.
- Discuss with students what would happen if a wild animal were unable to move. What if a domesticated animal could not move?
- Ask students if they know anyone who cannot move because of a disability.

Materials Needed for Each Group

- rubber bands
- plastic drinking straws
- long balloons
- stiff plastic (coffee can lid, milk container, etc.)
- large bowl or pan of water
- scissors
- stapler or paper clips
- plastic knife
- data-capture sheet (page 22)

Procedure *(Student Instructions)*

1. Fill a balloon half way up with water from the tap. Remove the balloon from the tap and hold the opening to keep water from shooting out.
2. Over a sink or bowl, open the balloon enough to stick in a plastic drinking straw to the bottom. Then hold opening to keep water from shooting out.
3. Using a rubber band, attach the neck of the balloon to the straw, making sure it is tight enough so water will not come out.
4. Bend the remaining part of the straw in half and attach a second rubber band so the straw will stay in place.
5. Cut plastic into two tail-shaped pieces. Place each cut-out tail against the neck of the balloon and attach with a rubber band. Then staple or paper clip the ends of the tail.
6. Put the plastic knife in between the two pieces of the tail, with the sharp end facing up. Then place the fish in the bowl or pan.
7. Lightly press your finger against the "nose" of the fish to keep it from moving from side to side. Next, push the tail of the fish from side to side using the knife and watch the fish swim.
8. After you have completed your fish and tested it, answer the questions on the data-capture sheet provided.

Extensions

- Have students find out if all fish move in the same manner.
- Have them compare the movement of fish to other aquatic animals and then to land animals.

Closure

In their animal journals, have students make a list of all the reasons animals need to move.

20

Do the Locomotion (cont.)

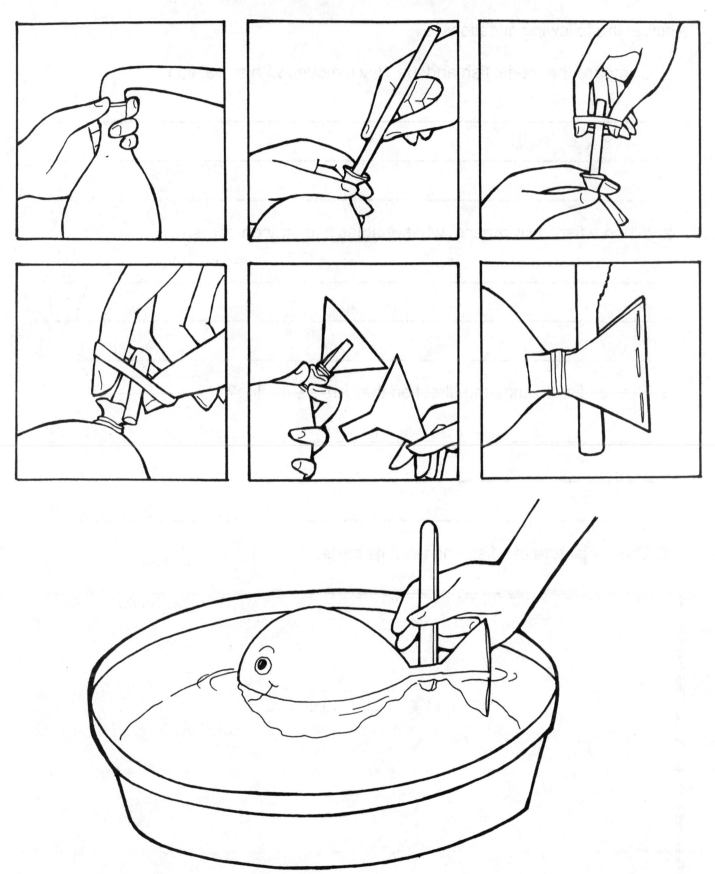

Do the Locomotion *(cont.)*

Answer the following questions.

1. Compare the model fish and the way it moves with a real fish.

   _____

   _____

   _____

2. When a fish is swimming, what enables it to stay on course?

   _____

   _____

   _____

3. How do fish change the direction they are swimming?

   _____

   _____

   _____

4. Draw a picture of a fish and label its parts.

Life Goes On

Questions

What is the life cycle of an amphibian? Without reproduction, why will a species eventually become extinct?

Setting the Stage

- Have students define the term *life cycle*.
- Discuss what happens to an animal during its life cycle.
- Ask students if they know the life cycles of any animals and list them.

Materials Needed for Each Individual

- colored markers
- scissors
- glue or tape
- pencil or pen
- data-capture sheet (page 24)

Procedure (*Student Instructions*)

1. Color in the different stages of a frog's life cycle.
2. Separately cut out the stages of the life cycle.
3. Glue or tape the stages in their correct order on the data-capture sheet.
4. Label each stage of a frog's life cycle on the data-capture sheet.

Extensions

- Go to the local pet store, get some frog eggs, and have students grow them in the classroom. When the frogs reach adulthood, either keep as classroom pets or release them back into nature.
- Have students study the life cycles of other animals. Then, at home, have students follow the life cycle of an insect.

Closure

In their animal journals, have students write a story about the life cycle of a frog.

Life Goes On (cont.)

Color, cut, and place frog stages in the appropriate order.

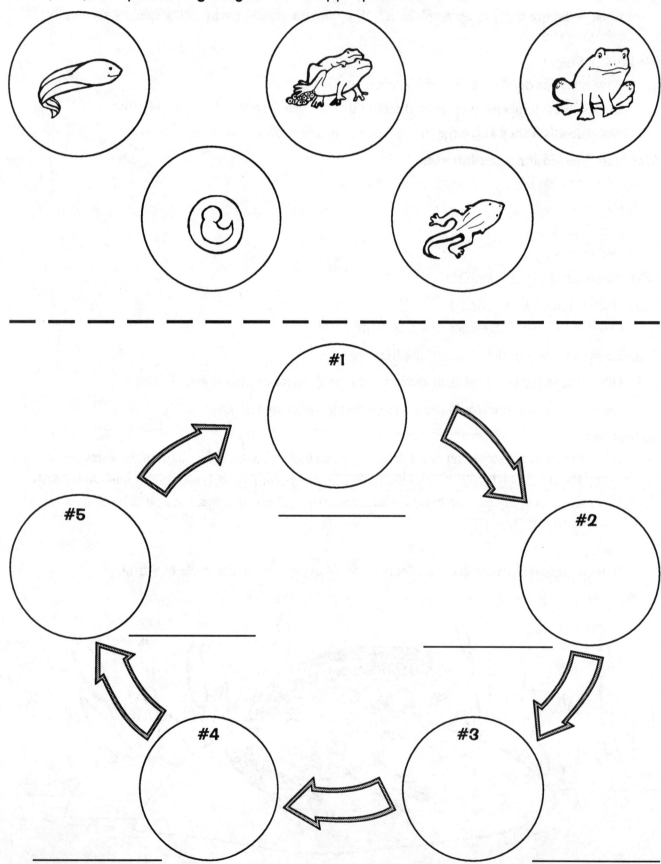

Eating in the Dark

Questions

   If an animal is to survive in the wild, how important are its senses? How do bats use echolocation to find food?

Setting the Stage

   • Review the five senses with your students.

   • Ask students if all animals have the same five senses. If not, what senses do they have?

Materials Needed for Each Group

   • water

   • small desk lamp

   • modeling clay

   • tin foil

   • data-capture sheet (page 26)

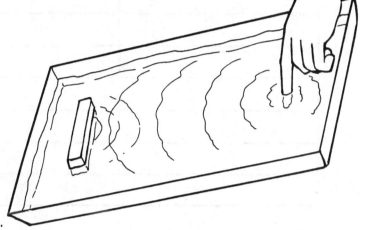

Procedure *(Student Instructions)*

1. Using a large piece of tin foil, make a tray about 12" (30 cm) long and about 6" (15 cm) wide. Make sure you make edges for the tray.

2. With the modeling clay, make a wall about 5" (13 cm) long and about 2" (5 cm) high. Then place the clay wall about 3" (7 cm) from the end of the tray.

3. Put the tray on a desk or table, and bend out the edges of the tray until they are sloping. Fill the tray with water but not so much as to spill over the side.

4. Next, put the desk lamp on the far side of the tray and turn it on.

5. Take one fingertip and dip it in the water on the side opposite from the clay wall. Watch the ripples move in all directions when you remove your fingertip from the water.

6. Finally, after the waves hit the clay wall, watch them return to where your finger was. This process simulates echolocation.

7. Using a stop watch, time how long the wave takes to return after you have removed your finger from the water. Record this information on the data-capture sheet provided.

Extensions

   • Discuss with students why a sense of hearing is so important to animals of the night.

   • Discuss with students any other senses that animals use at night to survive.

   • Discuss with students our most important sense for the night.

Closure

   In their animal journals, have students draw a picture of a bat using echolocation to catch a moth.

Eating in the Dark *(cont.)*

Fill in the chart and answer the questions below.

Student's Name	Length of Time for Wave to Return
Total=	

1. Add up the separate times and determine the average time a wave takes to return to where it started.

   _____

   _____

2. Once a bat receives a signal, what must it do in order to catch its meal?

   _____

3. Do you think bats hunt anything other than insects?

   _____

26

Just the Facts

Animals can be found almost everywhere in the world. They live underground, in the water, on land, and in the air. Some animals, such as manatees or spotted owls, live in only one or a very few special places where the environment is just right. Others, like mosquitoes and rats, are found almost everywhere.

ANIMALS LIVE AND GROW BEST IN A CERTAIN KIND OF ENVIRONMENT.

Some like it very warm, such as camels and scorpions. Others like it very cold, such as krill, penguins, and polar bears. All animals need a home where they can find food, a safe place to raise offspring, and protection from their enemies.

NOT ALL ANIMALS HAVE PERMANENT HOMES.

Many move from place to place with the seasons to satisfy different needs for food, warmth, and safety. For example, many birds migrate south in the winter. Some animals, such as salmon, return to the same place each year to have their babies. Animals called predators eat other animals. Since they usually have to follow their food and hunt for it, they do not have permanent homes, either.

ANIMALS LIVE WHERE THEY CAN HIDE FROM PREDATORS.

Many animals are camouflaged to blend into their environment. Others hide by holding very still or by appearing to be something else. Some hide in holes or go out to eat only at night when the darkness hides them.

MANY ANIMALS MAKE THEIR HOMES IN A GROUP.

For both adults and offspring, living in a group can provide protection from enemies. Many such groups are family groups, such as groups of humans, gorillas, swans, and beavers. Some animals live in family groups only during the mating season and while they are raising their young. The rest of the year they live on their own. Many birds live this way, forming pairs and building nests in the spring. Other animals, such as zebras, antelopes, and reindeer, live in very large herds all year round and move together to find food.

ANIMALS CAN BECOME EXTINCT IF THEY LOSE THEIR HOMES.

Many animals have lived in the world since the beginning of life, more animals than we will ever see again. For example, dinosaurs existed for over 150 million years before the world's environment changed so much they became extinct. Animals become extinct every day through natural and artificial means. The tragedy is that animals are disappearing at an alarming rate because of habitat destruction. Without clean and extensive forests, plains, mountains, and oceans, the animals that depend on these places for food and homes will die.

Everywhere You Look

Question

In how many different environments might you find animals living?

Setting the Stage

- Discuss with students the different environments in which they have seen animals.
- Discuss with students ways to observe animals without harming them.

Materials Needed for Each Group

- clipboard or lapboard
- paper
- colored pencils or crayons
- timepiece
- permitted areas for animal observation
- data-capture sheet (page 29), one per student

Teacher Instructions

- Divide class into groups of no more than four. Jobs should be divided among group members.
- The expedition leader makes sure all directions are followed.
- The timekeeper carries the timepiece and keeps the group within the time limits.
- The zoologist looks for animal specimens to observe. (All group members can be scouts!)
- The materials manager carries and distributes all necessary materials.
- The artist draws pictures of specimens seen in their environments.

Procedure *(Student Instructions)*

1. In your groups, travel to your assigned or chosen area of study. Each group will have fifteen minutes for their search for animals.

2. Inspect your area carefully. Look for animals in unusual places. Once they have been found, draw them in their environments on the data-capture sheet provided.

3. At the end of the time limit, return to the classroom and share pictures you have made of animals you found.

4. Discuss how each of the animals the class has found manages to have its needs met.

Extensions

- Have students research how geographical differences affect the types of animals that can be found in various regions of the world.
- Have students find out more about some of these and other animals living in unusual places: aardvark, dolphin, duckbill platypus, emu, kangaroo rat, narwhale, orangutan, penguin, sloth.

Closure

In their animal journals, have students describe or illustrate a story of an animal that has been moved to an area in which it cannot live.

28

Everywhere You Look (cont.)

Draw and write the names of every animal your group sees.

Move Over

Question

What will happen to animals in an environment where the carrying capacity has been reached?

Setting the Stage

- Have students define the term *carrying capacity*.
- Review with students four things an animal needs to survive. Discuss with students what might happen when a habitat becomes overcrowded.
- Ask students if this happens naturally or because of human intervention.

Materials Needed for Each Group

- classroom
- timepiece
- data-capture sheet (page 31), one per student

Procedure *(Student/Teacher Instructions)*

1. Have students sit close together on the floor in the front of the classroom. Use string or tape to mark off an area in which the students must remain.

2. For ten minutes, teach a lesson that the students will not like. An example of this might be anything having to do with difficult memorization.

3. During the lesson take note as to the interaction of the class while in the confined area.

4. After ten minutes, have students return to their seats.

5. Have students fill out the data-capture sheet.

6. Ask for volunteers to define the term *carrying capacity*.

Extensions

- Repeat the experiment by having students sit in a smaller area. Take students on a field trip to a place where animals can be observed in captivity and in the wild. Make observations to see if animal populations are under, at, or above the carrying capacity of the habitat.
- Have students do research on the effects of the carrying capacity on human beings.
- Have students explore the relationship between carrying capacity and "maximum occupancy" signs placed in cafeterias and meeting halls.

Closure

In their animal journals, have students draw a picture of an area under its carrying capacity and an area over its carrying capacity.

30

Move Over *(cont.)*

Answer the following questions.

1. How did sitting in a small place make you feel?

_____

_____

2. Was it uncomfortable sitting so close to the other students? Why?

_____

_____

3. Did you act differently than you would have if you were sitting at your desk? (The desk may be considered your regular habitat.)

_____

_____

4. Imagine you are an animal and you live in a small habitat with many other animals. Would you be able to survive in such a crowded place?

_____

_____

5. With so many animals living in one space, might there be a lack of proper amounts of food, water, and space?

_____

_____

6. Draw a picture of you and your classmates in your classroom carrying capacity.

Heading South for Winter

Question

Why do animals migrate during certain seasons of the year?

Setting the Stage

- Discuss with students why animals have to migrate.
- Ask students whether people migrated at anytime in history. Do any still migrate today?

Materials Needed for Each Group

- roll of string
- marking pens or crayons
- migration map
- data-capture sheet (page 33), one per student

Procedure *(Student Instructions)*

1. Cut string into several 8" (20 cm) segments.

2. Using the migration map, pick a migratory path and lay down a piece of string exactly along the path.

3. Mark the migratory path on the string using either a marking pen or crayon. The marked area represents the distance of the migratory path.

4. Using the mileage scale next to the map, figure out how many miles the bird has traveled during its migration. Write your answer on the data-capture sheet provided.

5. Repeat steps 1 through 4 for the other migration paths on the map and record your answers on the data-capture sheet.

6. After figuring out the distance traveled by each bird, try to calculate how long the migration took if the bird traveled at 25 miles (40 km) per day and 100 miles (160 km) per day.

Extensions

- Discuss with students what might happen in a bird's migration to prevent it from completing its trip.
- Take a class on a field trip to the wetlands.

Closure

In their animal journals, have students write about what it might be like to travel so much each year.

Heading South for Winter *(cont.)*

Complete the chart below.

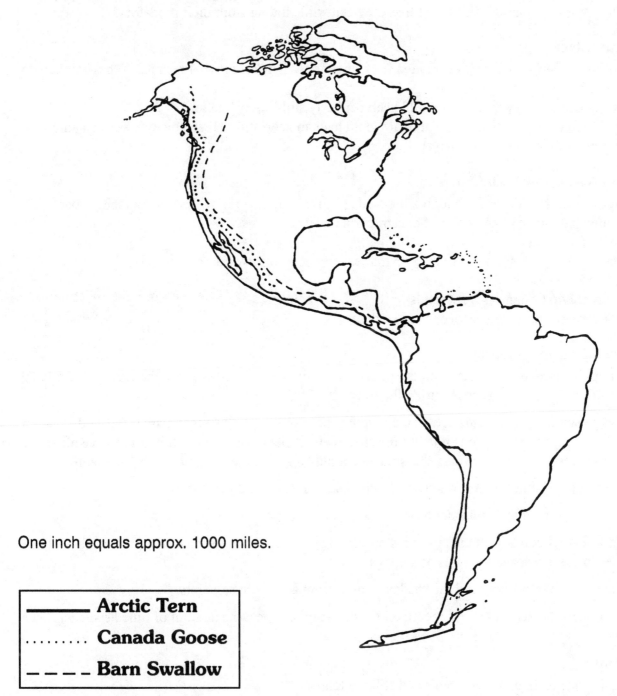

One inch equals approx. 1000 miles.

——————	**Arctic Tern**
··········	**Canada Goose**
— — — —	**Barn Swallow**

Bird	Distance traveled	How far at 25 mpd (40 km)	How long at 100 mpd (160 km)
Arctic Tern			
Canada Goose			
Barn Swallow			

Don't Move

Question

Why must prey animals keep as still as they can while hiding from their predators?

Setting the Stage

- Ask students if they have ever hidden from anyone. Where? For what reason? What did they do to hide?
- Ask students if they think they could keep perfectly still if they had to.
- Ask students why they think an animal would have to keep still. Have you ever seen an animal keep still? Why was it keeping still?

Materials Needed for Each Group

- large piece of cardboard 6 ft high x 3 ft wide (2 m x 1 m) covered with white butcher paper
- pointed hat, made of any color of construction paper
- box of push pins
- light source, such as swivel desk lamp that can be focused forward
- small table or desk
- timepiece that can measure seconds
- data-capture sheet (page 35), one per student

Procedure *(Student Instructions)*

1. Set up the lamp on the table, with the light focused on the wall. Make sure the table and the lamp are steady. You cannot move during the test.

2. One person at a time stands between the light source and the wall so that his\her full-body shadow is on the paper. Move the lamp until the shadow is as clear as possible. It helps to have other light sources turned off. **Note:** The student should be facing the wall, not facing the lamp.

3. The student should stand perfectly still, with hands at sides and feet together.

4. Place the pointed hat on his\her head.

5. Mark several points with the push pins on the edge of the shadow, such as the point of the hat, the sides of the arms, and the sides of the legs.

6. Time how long it takes until the shadow moves from any of those points.

7. As soon as the person moves, record on the data-capture sheet the amount of time he\she has been able to stand still.

Extensions

- Have students find out who can stand still the longest.
- Have students find out how far they move in any given amount of time. You may want to have them blindfold one another to see how this affects their movement.

Closure

In their animal journals, have students draw a picture of how they would look if they had to stand still while a predator was looking for them. Have them draw a picture of their predator looking for them.

34

Don't Move (cont.)

Fill in the chart and answer the questions below.

Student Name	Length of Time Standing Still

Who stood still the longest time?

_____

Why do you think that was so?

_____

_____

Who stood still the shortest time?

_____

Why do you think that was so?

_____

_____

I Need Some Company

Question

Why do certain species of animals live and work as a group?

Setting the Stage

- Discuss with students why some animals (humans) live together in family units.
- Discuss with students whether it is safer to be part of a large group.
- Ask students if a colony of insects can benefit one another.

Materials Needed for Each Group

- large wide-mouth jar
- bread or graham cracker crumbs
- eye dropper
- cheesecloth
- measuring spoons
- large, thick rubber band or string
- two large sheets of black construction paper
- masking tape
- water
- about 30 ants from same colony (Try to get a male and female.)
- sand
- large spoon
- rich soil
- baby-food jar
- sugar
- white chalk
- data-capture sheet (page 38), one per student

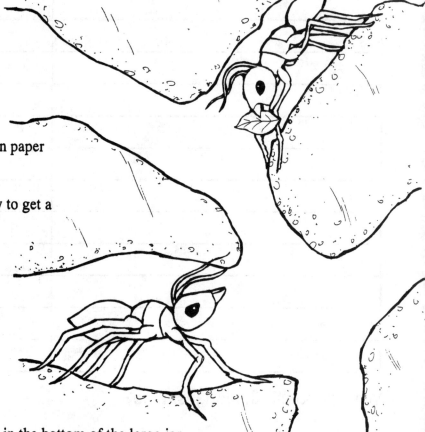

Procedure *(Student Instructions)*

1. Place the baby-food jar upside down in the bottom of the large jar.

2. Mix together an equal amount of sand and soil. Using the large spoon, put soil around the sides and top of the baby-food jar. Be sure to leave the sand and soil loose to form air pockets so the ants can breathe.

3. Mix 2 tablespoons (30 mL) of water with 1 tablespoon (15 mL) sugar. Fill the eye dropper and squirt drops into the soil. Add a handful of graham crackers or bread crumbs to the soil.

4. Carefully place the ants in the large jar. Cover the mouth of the jar with cheesecloth. Secure just under the rim with the large rubber band or string.

I Need Some Company *(cont.)*

5. Cover the outside and top with the black construction paper, using the tape to secure. This makes the ants think they are underground. Write the group's name with chalk onto the black construction paper.

6. Keep the ant observatories quiet by placing them in a safe corner of the classroom.

7. Each day for one week, remove the top piece of construction paper, feed the ants sugar and crumbs, and record observations on data-capture sheet. Re-cover with the construction paper.

8. After five days, remove all of the construction paper to see the amazing tunnels the ants have created. Record final observations on data-capture sheet.

9. When the study of the ant colony is complete, take the observatory outside and release ants in an appropriate place.

Extensions
- Have students study the similarities and differences of ant colonies and beehives.
- Have students compare and contrast animals that live in groups to animals that are solitary.

Closure
In their animal journals, have students pick an animal that either lives in a group or is solitary and have them tell why they would like to be that animal.

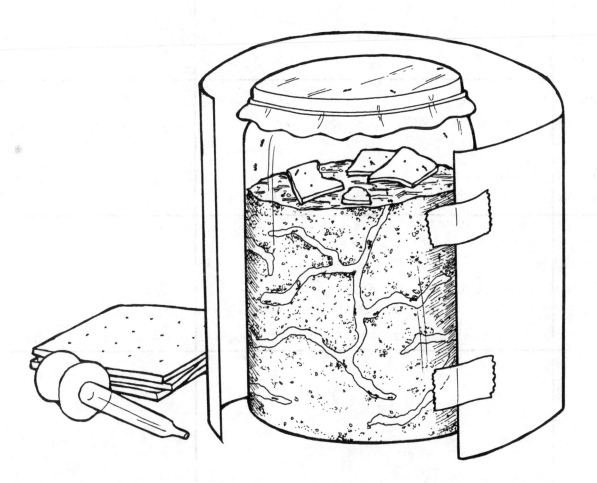

I Need Some Company (cont.)

Complete the observation journal below.

Ant Observation

Date	What Was Observed	Observer

Where Did They Go?

Question

What happens to the animals of a marsh when it is no longer there?

Setting the Stage

- Discuss with students the definitions of *endangered*, *threatened*, and *rare*.
- Discuss with students what happens to animals when their habitat is destroyed.
- Have students research why marshes were not given great priority until recently.

Materials Needed for Each Group

- colored pencils or crayons
- tag board
- scissors
- data-capture sheet (page 40), one per student

Procedure *(Student Instructions)*

1. Using colored pencils or crayons, color each scene on the data-capture sheet.

2. After coloring the scenes on the data-capture sheet, glue the entire sheet onto tagboard.

3. Using scissors, cut out each scene on the data-capture sheet.

4. Put the cards in order from the least amount of development to the most amount of development. Compare ordering with other groups.

5. After everyone has agreed on the order of the cards, discuss the importance of each card in class.

Extensions

- Discuss with your students why marshes are important.
- Ask students what we can do to save animal habitats.
- Have students write letters to a local congressman regarding an endangered species of their choice.

Closure

In their animal journals, have students draw a picture of what a marsh should look like.

Where Did They Go? *(cont.)*

Color and then cut out the scenes below.

What Was in My Dinner?

Question

Although loss of habitat is the leading cause of animal extinction, what else can cause animals to become extinct?

Setting the Stage

- Discuss and diagram the food chain with students.
- Ask students to make a list of things that could kill an animal. Compile a master list for the class.
- Discuss with students laws that have been enacted to protect animals.

Materials Needed for Each Group

- long rope
- paper cups
- animal food pieces, page 43; (breakdown of food pieces: 50% = plants, 33% = mice, 15% = snakes, and 2% = hawks)
- color one-third of all food pieces red
- a whistle

Procedure *(Teacher Instructions)*

1. Tell your students they are going to take part in a simulation called "What Was in My Dinner?"

2. Explain to students the different roles of the simulation. The mice eat the plants, the snakes eat the mice, the hawks can eat the mice or the snakes, and the hunter can shoot only the hawk.

3. Divide the class into mice, snakes, hawks, and the hunter. For a class of 25, try 16 mice, 6 snakes, 2 hawks, and 1 hunter. It is important that students remember what animals they are! To help, you can use name tags, colored bracelets, headbands, etc.

4. Use the rope to make a boundary for the simulation.

5. Pass out paper cups to students and tell them the cups represent the stomachs of their animals.

6. Explain to the students the object of the simulation is to collect in their cups the food their particular animal can eat.

7. The simulation should take place in rounds, each one lasting approximately two minutes. During each round the animals will enter the simulation at different times. Once the students enter the simulation, they remain until the end of the round. The mice will be the first animals to start the simulation. They will have 30 seconds to collect food. Then, the snakes will enter the simulation and will have 30 seconds to begin hunting for mice. Next, the hawks will enter the simulation and will have approximately 30 seconds to hunt for mice and snakes. And, finally, the hunter will enter the simulation during the last 15 seconds of the round and may hunt only for the hawks.

What Was in My Dinner? *(cont.)*

8. Spread out the food pieces within the roped area. Make sure students cannot see the symbols on the pieces before the simulation starts.

9. You are ready. Make sure students stay orderly and use the whistle to start and stop the simulation.

10. When the simulation is over, have students empty out their cups and count the food pieces they have. If they have fewer than two, they have starved to death. If they have two or more food pieces with a red line, they died of toxic poisoning.

11. Explain the ramifications of toxic chemicals in the food chain.

12. Repeat simulation as many times as you want. Have the students change roles each time.

Extensions

- Talk about the possibility of animals becoming extinct because of toxic poisoning.
- What kinds of things can be done to prevent the polluting of the food supplies with toxic waste?
- Have the class take part in a letter writing campaign to government officials about the issues of toxic poisoning in the food chain.

Closure

In their animal journals, have students draw pictures of endangered animals.

42

What Was in My Dinner? *(cont.)*

Student Rules for Simulation:

1. Listen to all directions.

2. Once inside the roped off area, you must stay there until the simulation is over.

3. You may pick up only the food pieces that your animal can eat.

4. Rowdiness will result in the end of the simulation.

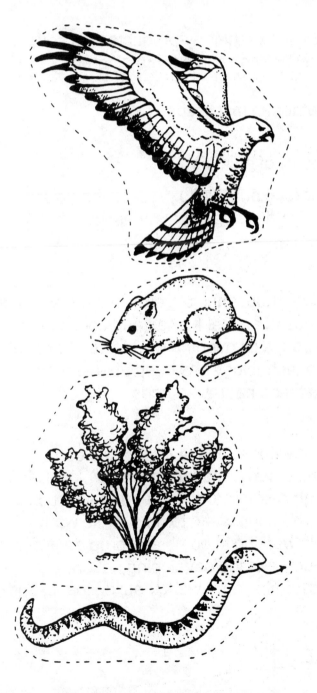
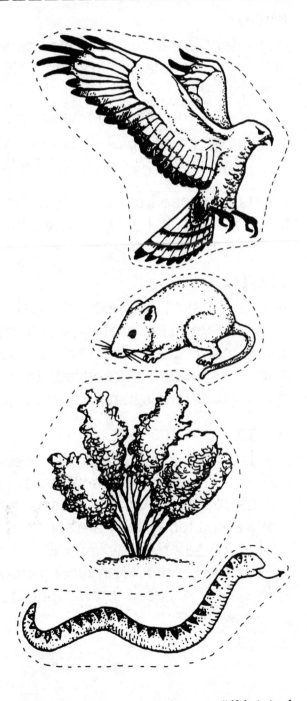

Just the Facts

Take a look around. Have you ever really noticed just how many ways animals and animal products are used? List or draw on a separate sheet of paper as many uses as you can. Then compare your ideas with the ideas of others in your class. Work together to come up with a master list of how animals are used. Animals provide us with many things. Without them it would be nearly impossible to live. Some of the things we obtain from animals are food, clothing, help with our work and transportation, companionship and enjoyment, population control, and environmental balance.

FOOD

Many people around the world use animals and/or their by-products as a source of food. Food obtained from animals can be broken up into three different categories.

1. *Meat:* consisting of muscle, fat, and other animal tissue
2. *Eggs:* made up of white and yolk.
3. *Dairy:* produced from the milk of a variety of animals

Foods produced from animals are much more expensive to process than plant food. As a result, they are more widely used in developed countries than in developing countries.

CLOTHING

Animal fur, skin, and wool have been used for thousands of years in the making of clothes. During the past few decades, the use of animal fur has and continues to come under scrutiny from animal support groups all over the world. Leather and wool are still used a great deal, but modern technology has been able to produce synthetic materials that are just as good as these natural sources.

WORK

Animals have been used to help people with work since the time of the early humans. They were used for transportation, to carry and pull loads, to plow fields, and as guards for various reasons. Although animals are not needed as much in these areas today, they are still used throughout the world to help make work easier and safer. Today you will find animals working in bomb and drug detection, helping the blind, and protecting crops. In some of the developing nations, animals are still used for transportation, performing farm work, hauling loads, and pulling wagons.

Just the Facts *(cont.)*

COMPANIONSHIP AND ENJOYMENT

Companion is defined as one who keeps company with another. Animals have been playing this role for generations. It has been said that "the dog is man's best friend." People around the world have befriended animals time and time again. The majority of households worldwide have had the companionship of an animal, whether it has been a goldfish, song bird, or a dog. We have always enjoyed having pets and always will.

POPULATION CONTROL

There are many ways to control the populations of animals. Over the years society has seen almost all of them. Hunting, poisoning, and trapping, which have been and are still used widely today, can be difficult and dangerous but are almost certain to take care of overpopulation problems. These methods have a tendency to be hazardous to people and cruel to animals, causing people to seek natural control methods. One natural control method puts the predator back into the wild, thus controlling overpopulation. Examples of this would be the use of cats to control rodent populations or spiders to control insect populations.

ENVIRONMENTAL BALANCE

Animals play a vital role in the health of the environment. They give the earth beauty and diversity. The animal kingdom lives within the checks and balances system. Certain species of animals are able to control the populations of other species. This is known as the food chain. For example, snakes keep rodent populations from getting too large, and in turn hawks and owls keep snake populations from getting too large. Animals also have the capability of genetic change needed for a new environment. If they are unable to change, eventually that species will become extinct. This is known as the process of "natural selection." Not only do animals keep their own populations strong, they also contribute to the growth of plants by pollinating, planting, and feeding without even realizing they are doing it. The role animals play in the environment is more important than some realize.

Yum!

Question

What physical change takes place in the making of butter?

Setting the Stage

- Discuss with students the three states of matter—solids, liquids, gases.
- Discuss with students and make a class list of the many different food products that have milk as an ingredient.

Materials Needed for Each Group

- 1 cup (250 mL) of heavy whipping cream (room temperature)
- small jar with a tight-fitting lid
- one marble
- colander
- cold water
- crackers
- salt
- data-capture sheet (page 47), one per student

Procedure *(Student Instructions)*

1. Place the whipping cream and marble into a jar. Screw on the lid tightly.

2. Once the lid is on tightly, you can begin to vigorously shake the jar, taking turns with the other students in the class.

3. After about ten minutes of shaking the jar, tiny round globules of butterfat called "butter granules" form from the cream and begin to stick together, making butter. Drain off the extra liquid which is now buttermilk and place the butter in the colander.

4. Press the pieces of butter together, place in the colander, and rinse with cold water several times.

5. Add some salt to the butter, mix it in, and spread it on a cracker to see how it tastes.

6. When you have finished tasting the butter, answer the questions on the data-capture sheet.

Extensions

- Have the class experiment by making other food products with milk products.
- Have a food tasting party with all new milk products your class made.

Closure

- In their animal journals, have students draw a picture of an old-fashioned butter churn.

46

Yum! *(cont.)*

Answer the questions below.

1. What physical change took place with the whipping cream?

   _____

   _____

2. How did this change occur?

   _____

   _____

3. Can you make the butter return to its original state?

   _____

   _____

4. With what other milk products can you create a physical change?

   _____

   _____

Is It Real or Is It Memorex®?

Question

Are natural materials stronger than those that are made synthetically?

Setting the Stage

- Discuss with students the reasons for developing synthetic materials.
- Make a class list of natural materials and then match those materials with their synthetic counterparts. For example, sugar = artificial sweetener and silk = polyester.
- Have the class bring examples of materials made from silk and materials that are synthetic.

Materials Needed for Each Group

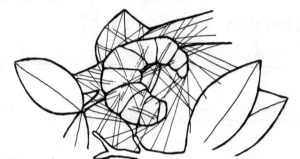

- four 12" (30 cm) strands of silk thread
- four 12" (30 cm) strands of polyester thread
- a spring scale
- an empty metal key ring
- data-capture sheet (page 49), one per student

Procedure *(Student Instructions)*

1. Tie one end of a silk thread to the end of the spring scale. Tie the other end of the thread to the key ring.

2. While one student holds the spring scale and a second holds the key ring, have a third student ready to watch the pointer to see at which degree on the scale the thread breaks. Have a fourth student ready to record the results.

3. When everyone is ready, have the first student hold the scale as steady as possible while the second student begins to slowly pull.

4. As soon as the thread breaks, the student watching the pointer gives the information to the recorder who records the results on the data-capture sheet.

5. Repeat the procedure with a polyester strand.

6. Repeat each experiment four times.

Extensions

- Have students research the history of silk and present a report to the class. Have them do the same thing with the history of polyester.
- Have students find out how silkworms make silk and then draw a diagram of the process. Have them find out the process of making polyester and then diagram it.
- Have students test other synthetic materials against their natural counterparts and see which is stronger.

Closure

In their animal journals, have students draw a picture of a piece of silk clothing they have designed for themselves. Have them describe how it makes them feel when they wear it.

Is It Real or Is It Memorex®? *(cont.)*

Record how much pull it took to break each type of thread. Then answer the questions below.

What Is Being Tested?		Silk	Polyester
Test 1			
Test 2			
Test 3			
Test 4			
Average Amount of Pull			

Which type of thread was stronger?

_____

Did you notice anything about the way either strand broke? Explain.

_____

_____

K-9

Question

Can animals' senses be beneficial to people?

Setting the Stage

- Discuss with students how animals can help people accomplish daily work routines.
- Ask students if there are jobs that animals because of their senses can do better than people. What are they?
- Ask students if there is any kind of special training required for animals to perform their jobs.

Materials Needed for Each Group

- blindfolds (one for each pair of students)
- food items that give off strong odors (cinnamon, garlic, onions, etc.)
- data-capture sheet (page 51), one per student

Procedure *(Student Instructions)*

1. Number food items from one to _?, depending on the number of items you have. Use the same numbering system on the data-capture sheet.

2. Pick a partner.

3. Whatever the number of food items, that many pairs should wait outside the room while the activity is being set up.

4. Place food items around the room.

5. Make access to food easy for blindfolded students.

6. When food items are set, pairs should enter with one partner blindfolded.

7. Blindfolded partners will explore the room, searching for foods, using only the sense of smell. When food items are located, the blindfolded partner should try to name them.

8. The other partner should record the information in the appropriate places on the data-capture sheet, as well as making sure his/her partner does not walk into anything or anyone.

9. Repeat the exercise until everyone has participated in the experience.

Extensions

- Brainstorm with students other experiences that can utilize the senses.
- Ask a police officer with a K-9 dog unit to come in and give a talk on how they are really used.

Closure

In their animal journals, have students write about what it was like to participate in this experience. How did it feel to only be able to smell the foods and not see them?

K-9 *(cont.)*

Write the food items next to the corresponding numbers. Then answer the questions below.

1. _____

2. _____

3. _____

4. _____

5. _____

6. _____

How many correct guesses? _____

How many incorrect guesses? _____

Was this exercise harder than you thought? Why? _____

_____

_____

_____

Where Is Water?

Question

Why can camels survive so long without water?

Setting the Stage

- Discuss with the class ways animals help us with transportation across the desert.
- Have students make a class list of animals that do not need much water to survive.
- Discuss with students all the possible places animals can get water.
- Have students do independent research on camels and share their information with the class.

Materials Needed for Each Group

- small potted plant
- small pot with soil and no plant
- tin foil
- one stick that is slightly longer than the plant

- two small plastic bags
- two rubber bands or twisty ties
- data-capture sheet (page 53), one per student

Procedure *(Student Instructions)*

1. Place the stick in the pot with no plant so it is the same height as the pot with the plant.

2. Using the plastic bags, place one over each pot. Close one bag at the point where the plant stem and the soil meet. Close the other bag at the point where the stick meets the soil. Use the rubber bands or twisty ties to do this.

3. Place both pots in an area where they will receive sunlight for at least a couple of hours.

4. Record observations on the data-capture sheet. Use the results of the experience to explain how animals can survive in places without visible signs of water.

Extensions

- Have students compare the amount of water needed by camels to the amount needed by other desert animals at certain times of the year. Ask students if there are any other animals that get water from eating plants. Make a list.
- Discuss with students what can happen to animals and people when they do not get the proper amount of water.

Closure

In their animal journals, have students draw a picture of a camel carrying supplies across the desert.

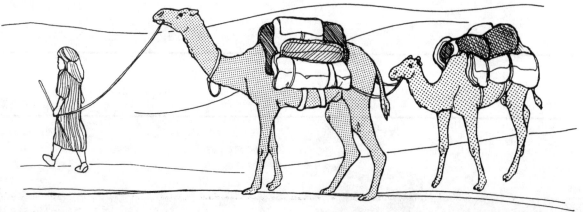

Where Is Water?

Answer the following questions based on your observations.

1. What did you observe by performing this experiment?

    _____

    _____

2. Is it possible to measure the water that condensed within the bag?

    _____

    _____

3. During certain times of the year, is it possible for camels to get all the water they need from plants? Why?

    _____

    _____

4. Why can camels sometimes go for months without drinking any water?

    _____

    _____

5. Draw a picture of a camel crossing the desert.

My Dog Rover

Question

How are pets different from each other?

Setting the Stage

- Discuss with students what animals need in order to survive (food, shelter, space, and water).
- Ask students what the difference is between wild animals and pets getting these needs?
- Have students determine a list of responsibilities for having a pet.
- Discuss why people have pets.

Materials Needed for Each Individual

- pen or pencil
- crayons or colored pencils
- pet (If students do not have pets in their homes, they can fill out the data-capture sheet using the pet of a relative, neighbor, or friend.)
- data-capture sheet (page 55)

Procedure *(Student Instructions)*

1. Take home data-capture sheet, observe a pet, and fill in appropriately.
2. Bring back completed data-capture sheet and compare information with other students.
3. Make a class list of the types of pets observed and compare similarities and differences.

Extensions

- Have students do extended research on their pets and share their new information with the class.
- Have a day for show and tell. Let the students bring in the pets they observed.
- Have a veterinarian come to the class and talk about animals in general.

Closure

In their animal journals, have students draw a picture of an unusual pet. Have them make up a story about what the pet might do and how they might take care of it.

My Dog Rover *(cont.)*

Complete this form as you observe your pet.

Your name: _____

Your pet's name: _____

Type of animal: _____

Group: *circle one*

    amphibian   arthropod (insect/spider)   bird   fish   mammal

    mollusk   reptile   other?

How much food does your pet eat daily? _____

Approximate weight: _____

Approximate height: _____

Number of legs: _____

Body color(s): _____

Body covering (feathers, fur, scales, etc.): _____

Photo or Drawing

The Spider and the Fly

Question

How are spiders used to help in the control of certain insects?

Setting the Stage

- Discuss with students some of the reasons natural methods are used to help control animal populations.
- Discuss with students the differences between using the natural and artificial methods of controlling animal populations.
- Have students make a master list of animals that would be used in controlling animal populations.

Materials Needed for Each Group

- one commercial or homemade terrarium large enough to keep insects
- vegetation for inside terrarium (plants, sticks, etc.)
- two garden spiders
- common house flies
- **Note:** For the purchase of spiders and flies, contact your local pet store and/or a biological supply company.
- pen or pencil
- crayons or colored markers
- data-capture sheet (page 57), one per student

Procedure *(Student Instructions)*

1. Using the terrarium, create a habitat that would be livable for flies and spiders.

2. On Day 1 place the flies inside the terrarium and give them 24 hours to get used to their surroundings. Record your observations on the data-capture sheet provided.

3. On Day 2 add the two garden spiders to the terrarium and continue daily observations of the terrarium. Record your observations on the data-capture sheet provided.

4. Continue observations throughout the week. On Day 5 make final observations and record what you see on your data-capture sheet. **Note:** This experience can be continued beyond a week.

Extensions

- You may want to have students do the experience again, using different insects.
- Have students research how spiders catch and eat their prey. Then share the information with the class.
- Discuss with students who might use these types of animal control methods.

Closure

In their animal journals, have students create a poem or story about what it would be like to be a predator searching for its prey.

The Spider and the Fly *(cont.)*

Complete the data-capture sheet below.

Day 1 observation:

Day 2 observation:

Day 5 observation:

Chickadees and Jays

Question

How are animal populations naturally kept in check?

Setting the Stage

- Review with students what a food chain is and draw several examples on the board.
- Have students brainstorm ways animal populations are controlled naturally within their habitats.

Materials Needed for Each Group

- one paper cup for each student
- beans
- one large bowl or bag
- an open area on school grounds (If none exists, improvise.)
- pen or pencil
- data-capture sheet (page 60), one per student

Procedure *(Teacher Instructions)*

1. Explain to your students they are going to be taking part in a simulation called "Chickadees and Jays."

2. Tell your students the different roles that can be played in this simulation. The chickadees collect beans (food) so they can raise their chicks, but the jays try to steal it away for themselves and their chicks. **Note:** The jays can only steal food from the nest, not the actual bird.

3. Divide the class into chickadees and jays (scrub jays west of the Rocky Mountains and blue jays east of the Rocky Mountains). For a class size of 25 or fewer, have all but three students be chickadees. For a class size of 25 or more, add one jay for every five additional students. **Note:** Additional adjustments may be necessary for atypically small and large classes.

58

Chickadees and Jays *(cont.)*

4. Give each student a paper cup to represent their nest.

5. Define the boundaries for the game.

6. Once the boundaries have been defined, give the chickadees one minute to hide their nests and return to a central staging area. While this is happening the jays must cover their eyes.

7. Place the beans in the central staging area. When all of the chickadees have hidden their nests they may begin taking beans (food), one at a time, back to their nests.

8. While the chickadees are taking beans back to their nests, the jays must cover their eyes and count to 30, after which they may start to follow the chickadees around and try to locate their nests. If jays find a nest, they are allowed to take what is inside it for themselves. Allow three to five minutes for this part of the game.

9. After the game is over, have all the birds count the number of beans left in their nests. Each bean represents a chick that was raised during the year. If no beans are left, that bird has died. Record the populations of birds on the data-capture sheet provided.

10. Discuss what happens when animals have an abundance or shortage of food.

11. Repeat simulations as many times as desired, having students change roles each time.

Student Rules for Simulation:

1. Listen to all directions.

2. Once inside the boundaries, you must stay there until the simulation is over.

3. Rowdiness will result in the end of the simulation.

Extensions

- Add toxic beans (colored) to the simulation and see how that changes the population count of the birds.
- Discuss with students the importance of predators in the food chain.

Closure

In their animal journals, have students draw a picture of baby birds in the nest, waiting to be fed by their parents.

Chickadees and Jays (cont.)

Fill in the information in the correct boxes.

Simulation	Number of beans collected by each chickadee	Class Total	Number of beans collected by each jay	Class Total
Simulation 1				
Simulation 2				
Simulation 3				
Simulation 4				
Simulation 5				

Answer these questions on the back or on another piece of paper after each simulation.

1. If each bean collected represents one chick being raised, how many chicks have been raised?

_____

2. How will the numbers of new chicks affect or not affect next year's food supplies?

_____

     60

Language Arts

Reading, writing, listening, and speaking experiences blend easily with the teaching and reinforcement of science concepts. In fact, science can be a focal point as you guide your students through poems and stories, stimulating writing assignments, and dramatic oral presentations. If carefully chosen, language arts material can serve as a springboard to an animal lesson, the lesson itself, or an entertaining review.

There is a wealth of good literature to help you connect your curriculum. Some excellent choices are suggested in the Bibliography (pages 95-96).

Science Concept: *the evolution of animals*

- There have been many stories written about how animals got certain physical characteristics, such as a trunk or tail or why they display certain behaviors such as sleeping all winter or buzzing, for example. Share with your students some of the stories you have heard or read. Then have your students write and illustrate their own stories of how an animal got a specific characteristic.

- Two possible headings are: 1) How the (the name of the animal) Got Its (a feature of the animal). 2) Why the (the name of the animal) (what the animal does).

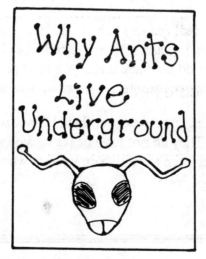

Language Arts

Science Concept: *Animals grow from tiny cells.*

- Read the following guided imagery to the class. Then discuss with students how they felt as they "grew." Use the guided imagery and discussion as a writing prompt.

Script

Imagine yourself to be small--very, very small. You are so small you can fit inside a hen's egg. And, that is where you are... It is dark inside the egg *(pause)* and wet *(pause)* and thick *(pause)* and gooey *(pause)*. You started as a tiny speck, but for the past couple of weeks you have been growing. Everything about you is growing--your eyes *(pause)*, your beak *(pause),* your feet *(pause)*, and your wings *(pause)*.

Even though you are inside an egg, you feel pretty safe. Your mother, the hen, sits on you all the time. She turns you every day. This way you stay warm all over. The yolk inside the egg gives you all the food you need to live and grow. You even have a little sac of air to breathe. The albumen, the white part of the egg, helps to keep you and the yolk safe by being a kind of pillow around you. You do get bumped at times by your brothers and sisters who are inside their eggs too. *(long pause)*

Well, it has been about three weeks now. You are getting a bit cramped inside your egg. You keep growing, but the shell doesn't *(pause)*. It is time to break out of there *(pause)*. Umph, peck, peck. Umph, peck, peck. Umph, peck, peck, peck, peck--there! You have made a little hole in the egg. But, keep working, working--you have got to get out of there fast *(long pause)*. FINALLY! You are out! WHEW! Boy, you are tired. That took almost a day to get yourself out. You can hardly walk straight. Oops, you slipped. And you have still got some of that sticky, gooey stuff all over you.

But now you can see your brothers and sisters chirping and peeping all around you. You cannot wait to meet all of them *(pause)*. *(suddenly)* Hey, hey, you guys! Wait, where are you going? Mom and everyone are leaving the nest without you. You start running after them and finally catch up. You wonder where mom is taking everyone. *(long pause)*

She has stopped! Mom has stopped! *(pause)* Why is she pecking at some dry, yellow stuff on the ground? And--pieces of egg shell? *(pause)* Oh, she is telling everyone that the yellow stuff is called corn. And, since chickens do not have teeth, you need pieces of shell or gravel in your stomach to help grind the food in your stomach into small pieces. Hmmm, that is interesting.

But what are those strange looking creatures over there? They walk on two legs like you do, but they do not look like chickens. They do not have beaks or wings like you do. *(pause)* One of them is carrying a basket and throwing corn to you. You wonder what they eat when they are hungry? Hmm.

Social Studies

Animals have played a significant role throughout history. Civilizations have thrived or declined because of animals. Cultures have been built around their use, and people have devoted their lives to working with them to make conditions in the world better in some way.

As you guide your students through lessons in history, geography, cultural awareness, or other areas of social studies, keep in mind the role animals have played. You will find it easy to incorporate the teaching and reinforcement of science concepts in your lessons.

Science Concept: *The sun's energy is found in everything we eat*

- Have your students play the game "Sunshine On Your Table" to help them understand how the energy of the sun gets to their table everyday.

Materials Needed for Each Group

- "Sunshine On Your Table" game board
- die
- colored game markers (enough for everyone in the group)

Procedure *(Student Instructions)*

1. Players select size-appropriate, easily identifiable markers.

2. All players roll the die to determine the order of play.

3. Beginning at **SUN**, each of you rolls the die to determine how many spaces you can move. Move marker that many spaces.

4. If you land on a space occupied by another player, that player is bumped back to the previous major space, such as **SUN, PLANTS, HERBIVORE, FARMER**, etc.

5. If you land exactly on one of the major spaces, you must go back to the next previous major space.

6. Once you know your die roll will take you past **HERBIVORE**, you have a choice of either going to **TABLE** by way of the **HUNTER-GATHERER** space, or the more conventional **FARM** to **RETAILER** way. If you choose the **HUNTER-GATHERER** way, you must (as you approach that space) roll the die until the number rolled places you exactly on **HUNTER-GATHERER**.

7. Once you have landed on **HUNTER-GATHERER**, another die roll will determine whether or not you can jump directly to **TABLE**. A roll of 2, 4, or 6 allows you to make the jump. A roll of 1, 3, or 5, however, means you must jump back directly to **HERBIVORE** to continue play.

8. The first player who gets to **TABLE** wins!

Social Studies *(cont.)*

Physical Education

What can be more fun for primary students then pretending they are animals, subject to the forces that make animals grow, thrive, and move? Here is an opportunity to let your students develop their knowledge of animals in a physical way.

Science Concept: *Animals have the use of many senses to help them survive.*

- The following game illustrates how bats, flying in the dark, use their ears as their eyes. This ability is called "sonar." A bat makes high-pitched squeaks as it flies. The sound bounces off anything in its path and echoes back to the bat. The echoes tell the bat what shape something is, how big it is, and where and how fast it is moving. The bat uses this information to home in on its prey.

Game Description

- In this game, one student (the bat) is blindfolded. Another student (the moth) is free to move around the predator. The rest of the class holds hands to create a ring (the walls of the cave) around them as the bat tries to catch its prey. In order to see its prey, the bat sends out a sound. It says, "**BAT**!" which "bounces off" the moth, who says, "**MOTH**!" in return. Using the "echo," the bat tries to locate its prey. As soon as the bat tags ("catches") the moth, the game is over. A time limit may be imposed by the teacher. However, a bat cannot survive if it can not catch its prey!

Math

The study of animals requires the use of math skills. The ability to measure, compare, and graph are just a few of the skills that can bring mathematics into your animal lessons.

- Teach or review the use of measuring tools (such as rulers with centimeters and inches to measure length).
- Have students practice reading and making charts and graphs.
- Provide opportunities for students to record data on a variety of graphs and charts. Teach the skills necessary for success.
- Encourage students to devise their own ways to show the data they have gathered.
- On an appropriate level, teach how to average test results.
- Challenge students to find mathematical connections as they study animals.

Science Concept: *Animals have a variety of ways of collecting food.*

- Have students work with a partner for this activity. When everyone has a partner, have them try to locate an ant hill with a trail of ants coming out. Then from the beginning of the ant hill, have each group measure out 10' (3 m) and mark it. Next, have the students put down a spoon of sugar and wait to see what happens. When they see an ant pick up a granule of sugar, time how long it takes for the ant to get back to the hill. Have the student groups repeat this four more times. Then help them to figure out the average ant speed.

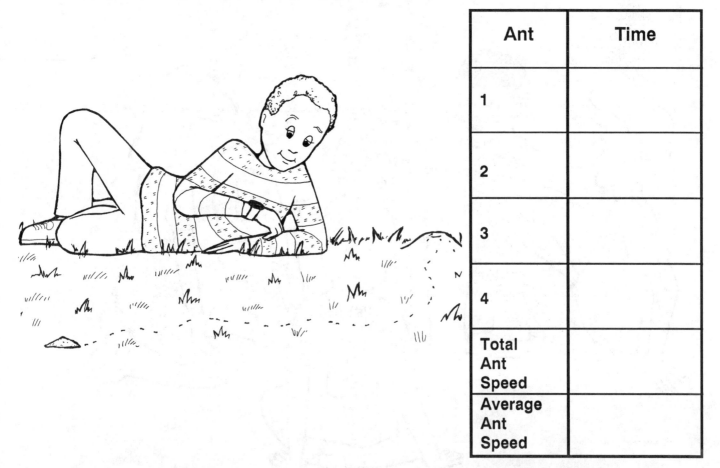

Ant	Time
1	
2	
3	
4	
Total Ant Speed	
Average Ant Speed	

You may want to follow this activity with the reading of *Two Bad Ants* by Chris Van Allsburg.

66

Art

Art projects using animals and animal products abound in the school and home. Your students will enjoy the "animal possibilities!"

Science Concept: *Animals have a variety of habitats*

- Have students use materials they have at home and in the classroom to create several different environments in which animals can live. Here are some ideas.

Display your finished environments for others to learn from and enjoy.

Music

Singing songs about animals, selecting orchestral numbers to "promote" the importance of animals, and making animal sounds in groups are just a few of the ways to integrate music into your animal-based lessons.

Science Concept: *Animals make sounds for many reasons*

• Have you ever been outside at night when all you can hear are the animals? Almost everyone has heard crickets and howling dogs. Animals can make such interesting sounds. Each is like a musical instrument.

• Create your own classroom symphony orchestra of animals. Decide which animal sounds you want in the orchestra. Then, assign students to make those sounds. You can have a symphony depicting the sounds of any type of animal environment you like. For example, the desert, the forest, or the rain forest can be depicted by your animal symphony.

• "Animals" making the same sounds should be in the same group. Then let the students take turns conducting the orchestra. They can make any kind of rhythm they want.

68

Observe

Before beginning your investigation, write your group members' names by their jobs on the lines below.

_____ Expedition Leader   _____ Stenographer

_____ Zoologist   _____ Transcriber

For thousands of years, people have used different kinds of animal hair to spin into thread and weave into cloth. Some kinds of hair work better than others. It is easier to make thread from hair that has a rough surface because the hairs can cling together.

Work together using the materials provided. Using a microscope or hand lens (of at least 30 power), look carefully at the hairs of a sheep, a human, and one other animal such as a dog, a cat, or a rabbit. Record below your observations about each type of hair, including a drawing of what you see. Then list three words that describe each type of hair.

Sheep	*Human*	

Descriptions: _____

_____

_____

Based on your observations, which of the three types of hair would be best to use to make cloth?

_____

_____

_____

Put your finished activity paper in the collection pocket on the side of the table at this station.

Communicate

Before beginning your investigation, write your group members' names by their jobs on the lines below.

_____ Expedition Leader   _____ Stenographer

_____ Zoologist   _____ Transcriber

On this table you will find eight pictures of animals to use to make a bar graph. Your graph needs to communicate at a glance how many animals are carnivorous, herbivorous, and omnivorous.

1. Sort the animals into three groups:
   meat eaters (carnivores);
   plant eaters (herbivores);
   and meat and plant eaters (omnivores).

2. Using the color key below, decide on a different color to represent each group of animals. Color the box next to the name of each animal group.

3. Count the number of carnivores, herbivores, and omnivores.

4. In your chosen carnivore, herbivore, and omnivore colors, color the appropriate number of lines on the graph corresponding to the number of these animals in each group.

5. Write the total below.

Color Key	Color	Number in the Group
Carnivore (C)	[ ]	_____
Herbivore (H)	[ ]	_____
Omnivore (O)	[ ]	_____

Total Number

Put your finished activity paper in the collection pocket on the side of the table at this station.

Communicate *(cont.)*

frog

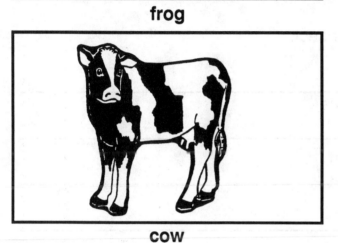

cow

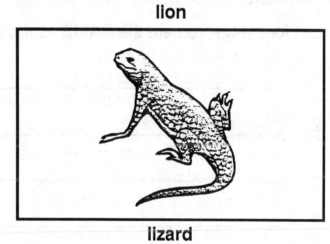

lizard

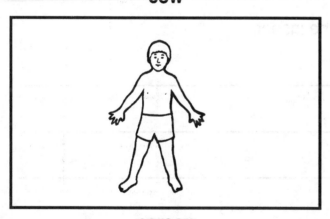

person

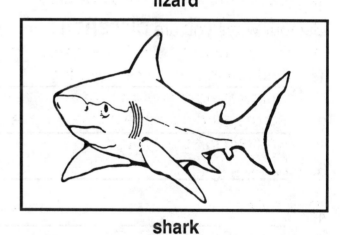

shark

rabbit

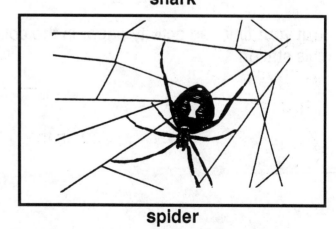

spider

Compare

Before beginning your investigation, write your group members' names by their jobs on the lines below.

_____ Expedition Leader   _____ Stenographer

_____ Zoologist   _____ Transcriber

At this station you will find an insect that your teacher has placed in a jar. Observe the insect carefully.

List four ways you are the **SAME** as the insect.

1. _____

2. _____

3. _____

4. _____

List four ways you are **DIFFERENT** from the insect.

1. _____

2. _____

3. _____

4. _____

Put your finished activity paper in the collection pocket on the side of the table at this station.

Order

Before beginning your investigation, write your group members' names by their jobs on the lines below.

_____ Expedition Leader   _____ Stenographer

_____ Zoologist   _____ Transcriber

At this station you will find four worms in a box. Place them gently on the table in order from shortest to longest. Measure each worm and record the length on the data-capture sheet. Draw a picture of each worm so that the picture is the same size as the worm. Gently move the worm around any way you need to so that when you draw its picture, the picture fits inside the box. Then return the worms to their box.

Worm #1 length:

Shortest

Worm #2 length:

Worm #3 length:

Worm #4 length:

Longest

Put your finished activity paper in the collection pocket on the side of the table at this station.

Categorize

Before beginning your investigation, write your group members' names by their jobs on the lines below.

_____ Expedition Leader   _____ Stenographer

_____ Zoologist   _____ Transcriber

At this station you will see a world map showing the continents. In a folder, your teacher has placed pictures of fifteen animals from all over the world. Decide which continent is the native home to each animal. Place the pictures on the continent. Then list the animal under the continent to which you think it belongs. Return the animal pictures to the folder.

CONTINENTS

Africa   *North America*   *South America*

_____   _____   _____
_____   _____   _____
_____   _____   _____
_____   _____   _____
_____   _____   _____
_____   _____   _____

Europe   *Australia*   *Antarctica*   *Asia*

_____   _____   _____   _____
_____   _____   _____   _____
_____   _____   _____   _____
_____   _____   _____   _____
_____   _____   _____   _____

Put your finished activity paper in the collection pocket on the side of the table at this station.

Categorize *(cont.)*

panda

kangaroo

lion

gorilla

turkey

penguin

armadillo

Andean condor

cobra

bald eagle

zebra

koala

llama

tiger

jaguar

Relate

Before beginning your investigation, write your group members' names by their jobs on the lines below.

_____ Expedition Leader   _____ Stenographer

_____ Zoologist   _____ Transcriber

At this station you will find three crickets in a small box covered with plastic wrap. You will notice there are air holes poked in the sides of the box. The plastic is there to keep the crickets from jumping out. Placed just over the top of the box is a flexible desk lamp with a 75-watt bulb.

1. Before turning on the lamp, listen for one minute and count how many times the crickets chirp. Record the number of chirps on the data-capture sheet.

2. Turn on the lamp. Make sure the lamp is not touching the plastic wrap. Count the number of chirps in one minute and record the number on the data-capture sheet.

3. Turn off the lamp. Count the number of chirps in one minute and record the number on the data-capture sheet.

Number of Chirps		
At Room Temperature	With the Lamp Turned On	With the Lamp Just Turned Off
Results:	Results:	Results:

At what temperature did the crickets chirp most? _____

Put your finished activity paper into the collection pocket on the side of the table at this station.

Infer

Before beginning your investigation, write your group members' names by their jobs on the lines below.

_____ Expedition Leader   _____ Stenographer

_____ Zoologist   _____ Transcriber

At this station you will find three sets of clues. You will read each set of clues and try to decide what animal that set describes. Write your guesses on the data-capture sheet.

Animal #1	**Animal #2**	**Animal #3**
has two wings	has golden fur	has suckers
has no backbone	has a backbone	has no backbone
eats plants	eats meat	eats lobster
lays eggs	gives birth	lays eggs
has two antennae	is a type of cat	has two pairs of beaks
hops	roars	is jet-propelled
has six legs	has four legs	has eight arms

- -

Our guesses:

#1 _____

#2 _____

#3 _____

Put your finished activity paper in the collection pocket on the side of the table at this station.

Apply

Before beginning your investigation, write your group members' names by their jobs on the lines below.

_____ Expedition Leader   _____ Stenographer

_____ Zoologist   _____ Transcriber

Use this paper and the other materials at this station to draw a picture of an animal that can live in one of the environments described.

Environment #1:
Cold, has snow, glaciers, ice flows, and Arctic Ocean

Environment #2:
Hot and dry, has sand, cactus, and very little water

Environment #3:
Hot and wet, has tropical plants, and lots of rain

Environment #4:
Cool to warm, has pine trees, lots of plants, and rain

Environment # _____

Put your finished activity paper in the collection pocket on the side of the table at this station.

Science Safety

Discuss the necessity for science safety rules. Reinforce the rules on this page or adapt them to meet the needs of your classroom. You may wish to reproduce the rules for each student or post them in the classroom.

Note to Teacher: When doing any animal investigation, be sure to caution your students to treat all animals with respect. They should not harm them in any way. They should also know how to recognize the poisonous animals in your area and know not to go near any animals they are uncertain about. Warn them not to approach any animal they see in the wild unless they have been assured of their safety by a knowledgeable adult.

1. Begin science activities only after all directions have been given.

2. Never put anything in your mouth, unless it is required by the science experience.

3. Always wear safety goggles when participating in any lab experience.

4. Dispose of waste and recyclables in proper containers.

5. Follow classroom rules of behavior while participating in science experiences.

6. Review your basic class safety rules every time you conduct a science experience.

You can still have fun and be safe at the same time!

Animal Journal

Animal journals are an effective way to integrate science and language arts. Students are to record their observations, thoughts, and questions about past science experiences in a journal to be kept in the science area. The observations may be recorded in sentences or sketches which keep track of changes both in the science item or in the thoughts and discussions of the students.

Animal journal entries can be completed as a team effort or an individual activity. Be sure to model the making and recording of observations several times when introducing the journals to the science area.

Use the student recordings in the animal journals as a focus for class science discussions. You should lead these discussions and guide students with probing questions, but it is usually not necessary for you to give any explanation. Students come to accurate conclusions as a result of classmates' comments and your questioning. Animal journals can also become part of the students' portfolios and overall assessment program. Journals are also valuable assessment tools for parent and student conferences.

How To Make an Animal Journal

1. Cut two pieces of 8 ½" x 11" (22 cm x 28 cm) construction paper to create a cover. Reproduce page 81 and glue it to the front cover of the journal. Allow students to draw animal pictures in the box on the cover.

2. Insert several animal journal pages. (See page 82.)

3. Staple together and cover stapled edge with book tape.

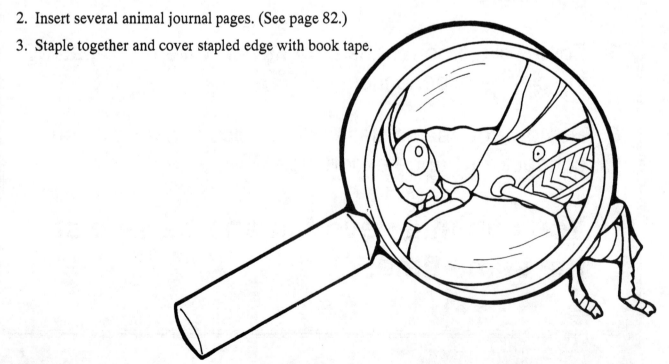

My
Animal
Journal

Name _____

Animal Journal

Illustration

This is what happened: _____

_____

_____

_____

_____

This is what I learned: _____

_____

_____

_____

_____

My Science Activity

K-W-L Strategy

Answer each question about the topic you have chosen.

Topic: _____

K - What I Already **Know:** _____

_____

_____

_____

_____

W - What I **Want to Find Out:** _____

_____

_____

_____

_____

L - What I **Learned After Doing the Activity:** _____

_____

_____

_____

_____

Investigation Planner *(Option 1)*

Observation

_____

_____

Question

_____

_____

Hypothesis

_____

_____

Procedure

Materials Needed:

_____

_____

_____

Step-by-Step Directions: (Number each step!)

_____

_____

_____

_____

_____

_____

_____

Investigation Planner *(Option 2)*

Science Experience Form

Scientist _____

Title of Activity _____

Observation: What caused us to ask the question?

_____

_____

_____

Question: What do we want to find out?

_____

_____

_____

Hypothesis: What do we think we will find out?

_____

_____

_____

Procedure: How will we find out? *(List step-by-step.)*

1. _____

2. _____

3. _____

4. _____

Results: What actually happened?

_____

_____

_____

Conclusions: What did we learn?

_____

_____

Animal Observation Area

In addition to station-to-station activities, students should be given other opportunities for real-life science experiences. For example, classroom animals can provide a vehicle for discovery learning if students are given time and space to observe them.

Set up an animal observation area in your classroom. As children visit this area during open work time, expect to hear stimulating conversations and questions among them. Encourage their curiosity but respect their independence!

Books with facts pertinent to the subject, item, or process being observed should be provided for students who are ready to research more sophisticated information.

Sometimes it is very stimulating to set up a science experience or add something interesting to the Animal Observation Area without a comment from you at all! If the display or materials in the observation area should not be disturbed, reinforce the need to observe without touching or picking up.

Assessment Forms

The following chart can be used by the teacher to rate cooperative learning groups in a variety of settings.

Science Groups Evaluation Sheet

Room: _____   Date: _____

Activity: _____

Everyone	Group									
	1	2	3	4	5	6	7	8	9	10
. . . gets started.										
. . . participates.										
. . . knows jobs.										
. . . solves group problems.										
. . . cooperates.										
. . . keeps noise down.										
. . . encourages others.										

Teacher comment

_____

Bragging rights for the group session: _____

_____

Assessment Forms *(cont.)*

The evaluation form below provides student groups with the opportunity to evaluate the group's overall success.

Cooperative Group Evaluation

Assignment: _____

Date: _____

Scientists	Jobs
_____	_____
_____	_____
_____	_____
_____	

As a group, decide which face you should fill in and complete the remaining sentences.

1. We finished our assignment on time, and we did a good job.

2. We encouraged each other, and we cooperated with each other.

3. We did best at _____

_____ .

4. Next time we could improve at _____

_____

88

Assessment Forms *(cont.)*

The following form may be used as part of the assessment process for hands-on science experiences.

Science Anecdotal Record Form

Date: _____

Scientist's Name: _____

Topic: _____

Assessment Situation: _____

Instructional Task: _____

Behavior/Skill Observed: _____

_____

_____

_____

_____

_____

This behavior/skill is important because _____

_____

_____

_____

_____

_____ .

Creating Science Projects

At the end of each lesson in this book, have students think about questions that were left unanswered or that they would enjoy investigating further. Help them transform their questions into science project investigations. The following example shows how the process that is used throughout the book may be used in the creation of science projects.

Example

Teacher: What did you learn in our science lesson today?

Student: Animals have ways to protect themselves from predators, including humans.

Teacher: What other questions do you have about the ways animals protect themselves?

Student: I want to know if certain colors will blend into an environment better than others.

Once students decide which question they would like to investigate, have them use the scientific method to do it. A project stemming from the above question may end up looking something like this:

Question

What color will be hardest to find in the grass on our school's playground?

Hypothesis

• The color that will be hardest to find will be green because it will be the same color as the grass, and a person's eyes will not be able to easily see the shape of the object.

Materials Needed for Each Group

• a variety of equal numbers of same-sized crayons without wrappers
• a designated section of playground
• data-capture sheet (page 91), one per student

Procedure *(Student Instructions)*

1. Determine the area to explore.

2. Scatter ten crayons of each color randomly across the area.

3. Give a small group of students two minutes to search the area. Urge them ahead of time to search the entire area.

4. At the end of the search, students turn in all crayons found.

5. Sort by color and count how many are found and compare to the number scattered.

6. Repeat the crayon search and data collection for each student in the group.

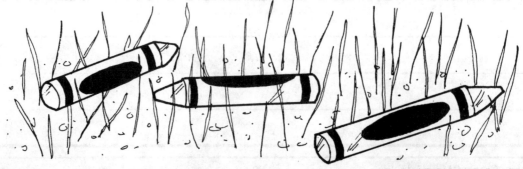

Creating Science Projects *(cont.)*

Results

Group Members: _____

	Crayon Colors	No. of scattered crayons	No. of crayons found
Color 1:			
Color 2:			
Color 3:			
Color 4:			
Color 5:			
Color 6:			
Color 7:			
Color 8:			
Color 9:			
Color 10:			

Which is the color hardest to find? _____

Which color(s) was/were found the least? _____

Which color(s) was/were found the most? _____

Conclusion *(Circle your conclusion and fill in the blank.)*

The results show that my hypothesis is (circle one) **supported.** **not supported.**

The color hardest to find is _____.

New Question

Do you think that the results would have been different on a playground that is different than yours?

Super Zoologist Award

This is to certify that

_____
Name

made a science discovery!

Congratulations!

_____
Teacher

_____
Date

92

Glossary

C

Camouflage—the ability to blend into the natural environment without being noticed.

Carnivore—an animal that eats the meat of other animals to survive.

Carrying Capacity—the ability of a habitat to sustain a population of animals for an indefinite period of time.

Colony—the same kinds of animals, plants, or one-celled organisms living together in a group.

Conclusion—the outcome of an investigation.

Control—a standard measure of comparison in an experiment. (The control always stays constant.)

Cycle—an interval of time that is regularly repeated.

D

Dissect—to cut apart and study internally.

Diversity—the biological difference between organisms worldwide.

Domestic—describing an animal that is no longer wild and can be used for human purposes.

E

Echolocation—a means for some animals to navigate their direction or to locate food. (Animals will release short sounds; when the sounds hit an object, they return as an echo, and the animal can locate it.)

Endangered Species—an animal or plant that is in immediate danger of becoming extinct.

Environment—all that is external to the living conditions of an organism.

Experiment—a means of proving or disproving a hypothesis.

Extinct—an animal or plant species that no longer exists.

F

Flyway—a migration route that is used by birds.

Food Chain—a sequence of organisms in which members of one level feed on those in the level below it and in turn are eaten by those above them.

H

Habitat—the environment in which a plant or animal can naturally be found.

Herbivore—an animal that eats plants in order to survive.

Hypothesis(hi-POTH-e-sis)—an educated guess to a question which you are trying to answer.

I

Interdependence—having to rely on other organisms in order to survive.

Investigation—to observe something and then perform a systematic inquiry in order to answer what was originally observed.

L

Life Cycle—the progression of an animal or plant from its birth to its death.

M

Marsh—areas of land that at least part of the year have waterlogged soil, support plants that need wet soil, and that are occasionally submerged or covered with water.

Migrate—to move periodically from one locality to another for feeding or breeding purposes.

Glossary *(cont.)*

N

O

P

Q

R

S

T

V

Z

Natural Selection—a process in nature whereby the organisms that are best suited to survive in a particular environment do, and all others eventually die (also known as "Survival of the Fittest").

Naturalist—a person interested in studying and watching living and nonliving organisms.

Observation—to notice or look at something.

Omnivore—an animal that eats both plants and animals in order to survive.

Predator—an animal that has to hunt down and catch its food in order to eat. Certain plants are also predators.

Prey—an animal that is killed for food.

Procedure—the series of steps that is carried out when doing an experiment.

Question—a formal way of inquiring about a particular topic.

Rare Species—an animal or plant that has a limited population or limited distribution worldwide. (It may or may not be threatened or endangered.)

Scientific Method—a creative and systematic process of proving or disproving a given question, following an observation. (Observation, question, hypothesis, procedure, results, conclusion, and future investigations.)

Scientific-Process Skills—the skills needed to be able to think critically. (Process skills include observing, communicating, comparing, ordering, categorizing, relating, inferring, and applying.)

Species—different kinds of animals, microorganisms, and plants.

Specimen—an individual organism taken from the whole, used in a study of that organism.

Sonar—See echolocation.

Synthetic Fibers—a fiber that is chemically manufactured. (Normally it is stronger than the natural fiber it is replacing; for example, silk is the natural fiber, and polyester is the synthetic fiber that is used in its place.

Threatened Species—an animal or plant whose numbers are depleting. The species is not in immediate danger of becoming extinct, but it may become endangered if the trend of depletion continues.

Variable—the changing factor of an experiment.

Zoologist—a scientist who studies animals.

Bibliography

Titles in the Let's-Read-and-Find-Out Science Book Series are valuable additions to your classroom library. For a list of current titles, write for a complete catalog.

Thomas Y. Crowell Junior Books
Harper & Row, Publishers, Inc.
10 East 53rd Street
New York, NY 10022

Here are some animal-related titles:

Animals in Winter	*Bats in the Dark*
Big Tracks, Little Tracks	*The Blue Whale,*
Camels: Ships of the Desert	*Corals*
The Eels' Strange Story	*The March of the Lemmings*
Spider Silk	*Twist, Wiggle, and Squirm: A Book About Earthworms*
What I Like About Toads	

National Wildlife Federation publishes several magazines, including **Ranger Rick, Your Big Backyard,** and **NatureScope.** Write for more information:

National Wildlife Federation
1400 16th Street NW
Washington, D.C., 20036-2266

Here are a few of the many other books that you may find helpful in preparing and presenting an animal unit to your class:

Aardema, Verna. *Why Mosquitoes Buzz in People's Ears.* Dial, 1975.

Arnosky, Jim. *Secrets of a Wildlife Watcher.* Lothrop, Lee & Shepard, 1983.

Back, Christine, and Barrie Watts. *Spider's Web.* Silver Burdett, 1988.

Bare, Colleen Stanley. *Sea Lions.* Dodd Mead & Co., 1986.

Baylor, Byrd. *Hawk, I'm Your Brother.* Aladdin, 1986.

Carle, Eric. *Animals, Animals.* Philomel, 1989.

 The Grouchy Ladybug. Thomas Y. Crowell, 1977.

 The Mixed-Up Chameleon. HarperCollins, 1984.

 The Very Busy Spider. Philomel, 1984.

 The Very Hungry Caterpillar. Philomel, 1969.

 The Very Quiet Cricket. Philomel, 1990.

Cherry, Lynne. *The Great Kapok Tree: A Tale of the Amazon Rain Forest.* Harcourt Brace Jovanovich, 1990.

Chief Seattle. *Brother Eagle, Sister Sky.* Dial, 1991.

Chinery, Michael. *Spider.* Troll, 1991.

Cole, Joanna. *A Snake's Body.* Trumpet, 1981.

Conyers, DeWitt. *Animal Poems for Children.* Western, 1982.

Daly, Kathleen. *Hide and Defend.* Golden Press, 1976.

Dewey, Jennifer Owings. *At the Edge of the Pond.* Little, Brown and Company, 1987.

Dorros, Arthur. *Ant Cities.* Scholastic, 1987.

Drew, David. *Animal Acrobats.* Rigby, 1990.

Eastman, P.D. *Are You My Mother?* Random House, 1960.

Eyewitness Books. Alfred A. Knopf. Many animal-related titles are available, such as *Bird, Butterfly & Moth, Dog, Insect, Fish,* and *Reptile.*

Eyewitness Juniors. Alfred A. Knopf. Geared more to a primary level than the Eyewitness Books series. Many titles available such as *Amazing Poisonous Animals, Amazing Mammals, Amazing Spiders,* and *Amazing Frogs and Toads.*

Bibliography *(cont.)*

Fleischman, Paul. *Joyful Noise*. Trumpet, 1988.

Hall, Howard. *The Kelp Forest*. Blake, 1990.

Harlan, Jean. *Science Experiences for the Early Childhood Years*. Macmillan, 1992.

Hornblow, Leonora and Arthur. *Insects Do the Strangest Things*. Random House, 1990.

Howe, James. *I Wish I Were a Butterfly*. Gulliver, 1987.

Lindbergh, Reeve. *The Midnight Farm*. Dial, 1987.

Lovett, Sarah. *Extremely Weird Insects*. John Muir Publications, 1992.

McGrath, Susan. *Saving Our Animal Friends*. National Geographic Society, 1986.

O'Hagan, Caroline. *It's Easy to have a Caterpillar Visit You*. Lothrop, Lee & Shepard Books, 1980.

Oppenheim, Joanne. *Have You Seen Birds?* Scholastic, 1986.

O'Toole, Christopher. *Discovering Ants*. Bookwright Press, 1990.

Parker, Steve. *Insects*. Dorling Kindersley, Inc., 1992.

Pope, Joyce. *Do Animals Dream?* Viking Kestrel, 1986.

Powzyk, Joyce. *Animal Camouflage, a Closer Look*. Bradbury Press, 1990.

Prelutsky, Jack. *The Random House Book of Poetry for Children*. Random House, 1983.

Russell, Helen Ross. *Ten-Minute Field Trips: Using the School Grounds for Environmental Studies*. J.G. Ferguson, 1973.

Sclezka, J. *The True Story of The Three Pigs*. Viking Press, 1990.

Simon, Seymour. *Animal Fact, Animal Fable*. Crown, 1979.

Taylor, Barbara. *The Animal Atlas*. Random House, 1992.

Van Allsburg, Chris. *Two Bad Ants*. Houghton Mifflin, 1988.

Yolen, Jane. *Owl Moon*. Philomel, 1987.

Spanish Titles

Berenstain, S. *El Bebe de Los Osos Berenstain (The Berenstain Bears' New Baby)*. Random House, 1990.

Carle, E. *La Oruga Muy Hambrienta (Very Hungry Caterpillar)*. Putnam, 1989.

Pallotta, J. *Cuenta Los Insectos Feitos (The Icky Bug Counting Book)*. Charlesbridge, 1992.

Scienzka, J. *La Verdadera Historia De Los Tres Creditos (The True Story Of The Three Pigs)*. Viking Press, 1990.

Torres, L. *Gorrion Del Metro (Subway Sparrow)*. Farrar, Strauss, & Giroux, 1993.

Technology

Agency for Instructional Technology. *Animal Adaptations: Why Do Zebras Have Stripes?* Available from ATI, (800)457-4509. video

Bean, Norman. *All About Animals: Insects*. Available from AIMS Media, (800)367-2467. laser videodisc

Burroughs, Jim. *A First Look at Mammals, All About Mammals, A First Look at Birds,* and *All About Birds*. Available from AIMS Media, (800)367-2467. laser videodisc

Carlson, Mike. *Animals Are Different And Alike*. Available from Cornet/MTI Film & Video, (800)777-8100. video

Cornet/MTI. *Animals Of A Living Reef, Animals Of North America,* and *Animals Of South America*. Available from Cornet/MTI Film & Video, (800)777-8100. video

Disney Educational Productions. *San Diego Zoo*. Available from Cornet/MTI Film & Video, (800)777-8100. video

January Productions. *Reptiles*. Available from CDL Software Shop, (800)637-0047. software